MASCULINITY
AT THE
CROSSROADS

MASCULINITY AT THE CROSSROADS

GARY J. OLIVER, Ph.D.

MOODY PRESS
CHICAGO

ISBN: 0-8024-3812-5

1 3 5 7 9 10 8 6 4 2

Printed in the United States of America

When I was in high school, a joke was circulating about President Lyndon Johnson and his "Great Society." It went something like this:

"Do you know what Lyndon Johnson has in common with Christopher Columbus?"

"No!"

"Well, when Columbus started out, he didn't know where he was going. When he got there he didn't know where he was. When he came back he didn't know where he had been. And he did all of this on borrowed money."

Unfortunately, the same thing could be said about many men today. We're not sure where we are going, we're not sure where we are, and we're not sure where we have been. And we are doing it all on borrowed time, energy, relationships, and money.

Men in America have been tossed around by the winds of technological and social change. The winds of change have blown us off course and many of us are like ships without rudders. Our experiences range from conflict and confusion to chaos and crisis. We know we've got to go in some direction, but we aren't clear about what direction to take.

When I first met Ted he was the kind of man I've just described. Our first contact came in the form of a note he handed to me. Attached to the note was a copy of a test he had taken earlier that day. It was part of a workshop I was teaching for pastors on how to increase their effectiveness in counseling. His short note read: "As you will see in the test, I have some serious problems with my self-image. I've known this for a long time and the testing pointed out to me that the problem is more severe than I had realized. I know that it is handicapping my ministry and my effectiveness as a witness for Jesus Christ. I'm praying that with God's help and your counsel these matters can be corrected."

Early the next week I received a phone call from Ted. "This is one of the most difficult things I've ever done, but I know my problems aren't going to magically disappear and I need some help." Ted was the pastor of a growing evangelical church. He had been reared in a Christian home, attended Christian schools, and graduated from a theologically conservative seminary.

We began meeting, and he continued his story: "When I first entered the ministry I knew there would be struggles with elders, deacons, and members of the congregation. I expected to face problems with finances. I knew there would be situations in which I wouldn't have the answer and would need to reach out to other leaders for advice. I felt that I had realistic expectations and was well trained to handle those kinds of problems."

At this point he paused, took a deep breath, and looking me straight in the eyes said, "What I didn't expect, what I wasn't ready for, what seminary hadn't prepared me for were the struggles I would battle *within* myself." Ted went on to share some of his struggles with worry, self-doubt, feelings of inadequacy and insecurity, and fear of failure.

"In school I learned a lot about eschatology, ecclesiology and soteriology, but I didn't learn much about what it means to be a man. I didn't learn how to understand and deal with my emotions." Up to this point Ted had dealt with these concerns by working and eating. He had become a workaholic, putting in an average of sixty hours a week. The first time I saw Ted, he was about sixty pounds overweight. That's a lot of extra weight for a man who is 5'8".

With all of his heart Ted wanted to be a good son, husband, father, friend, and pastor. He had exerted enormous amounts of physical and emotional energy striving for his lofty goals. But what I saw before me was a middle-aged man who was broken, confused, discouraged, and exhausted. "I feel lost. I'm no longer sure what it means to be a real man. I'm not sure where to start. And worst of all, I'm not sure that I care."

I assured Ted that he did care. If he didn't, he wouldn't have made an appointment to see me. I also told him that through his prayer and seeking God's guidance he had already started. His being willing to become vulnerable and to open his heart to men was another step on the road to healing and health.

In a later session we talked about how boys become men. I shared with him that much of how we see ourselves can be influenced by the way the significant people in our lives see us. We discussed how he thought his mother and father viewed him. I asked him to think a bit more about that and told him we would discuss it at our next session.

The next week he started by saying, "Dr. Oliver, as I thought about it, I'm amazed at the power of the labels I received from parents and others. My folks have always stamped me with the label 'lazy,' and I always feel that I'm lazy. No matter if I work twelve hours and then watch TV for one hour, I see myself as lazy. My father used to say, 'You're so lazy you stink.' That still haunts me. Even when I worked hard as a child, I was never praised or rewarded. I would always be compared to my father who 'Back when I was a boy' worked harder than superman himself."

Ted's father was a good and honest man. He was an elder in their church. He was a hard worker. Unfortunately, he worked so many hours that he wasn't home much. The majority of the parenting Ted received came from his mother. "I know my dad loved me, but when I think of my dad when I was growing up, I think of someone I could never please. Someone who was always encouraging me to do more, do better, and work harder."

Several weeks later Ted dropped a handwritten note off at my office: "In our last session you talked about how so many people do things in order to be loved, and they try to read their parents and others to sense what they want—that truly describes me. *I have spent most of my life trying to please teachers, friends, and parents and trying to shape my life by their expectations.* I went through all of my schooling, including seminary, harboring these underlying motivations, apparently trying to find a deep sense of security and love."

Within nine months Ted had lost more than thirty-five pounds, was working between forty and fifty hours per week, was spending quantity and quality time with his wife and three young children and "am experiencing the abundant life that Christ talks about and that for many years I had spoken about." Ted said, "I am learning what it means to be a man, a godly man."

The story of Ted could be that of hundreds of men that I've worked with. It might be similar to *your* story. His story illustrates some of the issues men are struggling with today. Many of the men I have counseled are bright, intelligent men who love the Lord, read the Word, are active in their local churches, and want to grow. Yet they find themselves stuck in the rut of struggles they don't understand and aren't sure how to deal with.

Ronald F. Levant has written,

> To many men, particularly in mid-life, the question of what it means to be a man today is one of the most persistent unresolved issues in their lives. Raised to be like their fathers, they were mandated to become the good provider for their families, and

to be strong and silent. They were discouraged from expressing vulnerable and tender emotions, and required to put a sharp edge around their masculinity by avoiding anything that hinted of the feminine. Unlike their sisters, they received little, if any, training in nurturing; in being sensitive to the needs of others or empathic with their voices. On the other hand, they received lots of training in problem-solving, logical thinking, risk-taking, staying calm in the face of danger, and assertion and aggression.[1]

Many of us are like Ted. As young boys we were taught the rules: Work long and hard. Ignore your emotions. Seek achievement and status. Be self-reliant. Don't let anyone push you around. Don't have close male friends. Avoid anything that could even come close to looking like or being mistaken for femininity. Maintain an emotionally distant and nonrelational attitude toward sexuality. Most of us learned these lessons well. Too well!

The Price of Power

As Christian men we want to honor God and obey Jesus Christ in our personal relationships. Many men wonder how their faith should affect their sense of masculinity. By virtue of being a male you are facing a crisis of identity. Every American male is. What do I mean by crisis? Webster defines crisis as "an emotionally significant event or radical change of status in a person's life . . . an unstable or crucial time whose outcome will make a decisive difference for better or worse."

We men are reeling from the challenges and changes that have assaulted us in the past twenty years. We have been bombarded on every side by conflicting and contradictory signals from our mothers and fathers, our wives, and from other women, children, pastors, friends, and peers. On the one hand, we are told, "Be strong, but don't be macho." On the other hand, we hear, "Be sensitive, but don't be a wimp." It wouldn't be so hard if there were an objective Macho-Wimp scale we could turn to for help in evaluating attitudes and behavior. Unfortunately there isn't.

Herb Goldberg has effectively described the crisis facing today's male:

> In recent years there has been a dramatic change in the perception and functioning of the male in our culture. It has become increasingly clear that the gender orientation known as masculinity has serious and troubling limitations and, con-

sequently, has put the male clearly in crisis. He is accused of being chauvinistic and oppressive. He is fearful of abandonment by his increasingly autonomous and powerful woman. He is burning himself out physically and emotionally in pursuit of a success trip and other goals whose fruits are all too often questionable and meager. He hears and reads endless discussions about his declining sexual performance and increasing "dysfunction," supposedly caused by women's new assertiveness. He is lacking a support system with other men to help him through these crises, and he possess little insight into the causes of what is happening to him and has few inner resources to draw on for nourishment during the difficult periods. He is truly a cardboard goliath, unable to flow self-caringly with the changing social scene.[2]

Most men have pursued excellence as breadwinners, work machines, and performers; meanwhile, everything else has suffered. In recent years it's become clear that growing up male can be hazardous to your health! In the past year I've collected a few statistics that you probably haven't heard before. The list of male-specific inequities, inferiorities, and wounds is much more extensive than I ever realized:

- Infant boys receive fewer demonstrative acts of affection from their mothers and are touched less than infant girls.

- Not only are boys touched less frequently by their mothers than girls, they are talked to less, and for shorter periods of time.

- Infant boys are more likely to be held facing outward, toward the world and other people. Girls are held inward, toward the security, warmth, and comfort of the parent.

- Infant boys crawl, sit, and speak later and tend to cry more, yet girls are more likely to get a positive response when crying for help than boys.

- When a child complains of a minor injury, parents are quicker to comfort girls than boys.

- Since boys are considered by most people to be emotionally tougher than girls, they are more often reprimanded in front of the whole class for misbehavior, whereas girls are more likely to be taken aside and spoken to more softly.

- Young boys are admitted to mental hospitals and juvenile institutions about seven times more frequently than girls of similar age and socioeconomic background.

- Boys are much more likely to suffer from a variety of birth defects. Boys are more prone to schizophrenia. They suffer a higher incidence of mental retardation. In fact, there are about 200 genetic diseases that affect only boys, including the most severe forms of muscular dystrophy and hemophilia.

- Boys are twice as likely as girls to suffer from autism and six times as likely to be diagnosed as having hyperkinesis.

- Boys stutter more and have significantly more learning and speech disabilities than girls. Some research suggests that dyslexia is found in up to nine times as many boys as girls.

- When boys become teenagers they are told they must be prepared to be mutilated or die in order to protect women and children and the ideologies of their nation.

- In Vietnam 8 women and more than 58,000 American men died.

- Men have a 600 percent higher incidence of work-related accidents than women, and men die from work-related injuries approximately 20 to 1 over women.

- Whereas the government compiles many statistics on the needs of working mothers, none are kept on

15

behalf of fathers, including the special needs of the nearly 3 million men who are single parents.

- Suicide rates are about four times higher for men than women.
- Men make up about 80 percent of all homicide victims, are victims of about 70 percent of all robberies, and make up 70 percent of all other victims of aggravated assaults.
- A man's life expectancy is as much as nine years less than a woman's.
- There are 29,000 female prisoners in the United States and 553,000 male prisoners.
- Ninety-nine percent of the prisoners on death row are males.
- Of the 157 people executed since the death penalty was reinstated in 1973, only one was female.[3]

Now let's go back into your teen years, a time of alternating tension and fun. Whether you regard your high school years as "Happy Days" or a fearful "One Day at a Time," you need to know the truth about that period of life: your teen years were when you began to experience the wounds of your masculine crisis. Consider these four areas of male tension we faced, beginning as teenaged boys: fear, challenging moral standards, a reluctance to help, and show-

16

ing negative and antisocial behavior. In each of these areas, boys struggle more than girls in adjusting to the pressures around them. The following material is adapted from an article in *Source* journal, which summarized research from *The Quicksilver Years: The Hopes and Fears of Early Adolescence.*[4]

FEAR

With one exception the things boys fear more than girls center on physical force or some kind of self-destructive or other-destructive activity, whereas many of girls' greatest fears center on loss or disturbance of friend relationships. Boys do, however, worry more than girls about not getting a good job when they are older.

High on the boys' list is a disturbing trio of worries more real to them than to girls: fear of getting beaten up at school, fear of the possible nuclear bombing of the U.S., and fear that their friends may get them into trouble. Next is another trio of fears with some of the same violent undertones, although here the difference between boys and girls is less: the destructiveness of a parent's drinking, physical abuse by a parent, and fear of suicide.

MORAL STANDARDS

Boys' views of morality also differ from those of girls. Fewer boys than girls think it is wrong to disrupt a classroom, to take something from a store without paying for it, to lie to parents, to use alcohol, or to practice racial discrimination. The level of approval of these antisocial behaviors among boys suggests a disturbing disregard of honesty, coupled with the belief that one's own welfare and interests should always come first.

RELUCTANCE TO HELP

Boys lag behind girls in acts of generosity to others. They are far less likely than girls to initiate and carry out an activity that helps others (e.g., mowing lawns or shoveling walks) without pay. About half of all young adolescents surveyed said they would stop to help a crying child on a playground or to help pick up the contents of a dropped bag of groceries, but the percentage of boys is markedly smaller than that of girls.

NEGATIVE BEHAVIORS

Boys carry off the prize for frequency of participation in almost every kind of negative behavior measured in our study of early adolescents. Whether vandalism, beating up someone, gang fighting, or theft, the percentage of boys admitting participation markedly exceeds that of girls. In vandalism and beating up someone, boys' percentages are about twice that of girls.

In all areas of drug use, such as frequency of drinking, being drunk, or use of marijuana, boys' participation is higher. The only exception is cigarettes, where girls win the dubious honor.

A study by the Search Institute of the drug use and drug-related attitudes of 11,000 Minnesota public school students provided essentially the same results: boys dominate the negative side of the comparison.[5]

Growing Up Is Hard to Do

In our society tremendous pressure is placed on boys to "Grow up!" Frank Pittman graphically describes this pressure:

> As a guy develops and practices his masculinity, he is accompanied and critiqued by an invisible male chorus of all the other guys who hiss or cheer as he attempts to approximate the masculine ideal, who push him to sacrifice more and more of his humanity for the sake of his masculinity, and who ridicule him when

he holds back. The chorus is made up of all the guy's comrades and rivals, all his buddies and bosses, his male ancestors and his male cultural heroes, his models of masculinity—and above all, his father, who may have been a real person in the boy's life, or may have existed for him only as the myth of the man who got away.[6]

But what does it mean to "Grow up!"? *How* does a boy become a man? *When* does a boy become a man? Why is what should be so easy, so difficult? When I was in junior high I thought that once I got taller, got a deeper voice, grew body hair, had to shave, was able to drive, had a job and earned my own money, and was able to get a girl, that I would be a man. Was I wrong!

In our culture the social expectations and definitions are contradictory and ambiguous, there are few healthy male role models with which to identify, and there are no clearly established rites of passage into manhood.

Due to changing concepts of masculinity, new demands and expectations are being made on men in our society. Without available fathers, rites of passage, or positive male role models, the transition from boyhood to manhood has become increasingly difficult, if not impossible. Many of today's men struggle with feelings of confusion, guilt, vulnerability, and inadequacy. Painful and emotionally wounding childhoods have left many men silently enduring anger, grief, and despair.

Unfortunately, most men don't understand these emotions. They never learned how. And they don't know what to do with them. So most men do what every red-blooded American male before them has done. They do what they have seen modeled at home, at school, on television, and in the movie theater. They take their messy, uncomfortable, and misunderstood emotions and stuff, repress, suppress, deny and ignore them . . . or they let their emotions control them and become overwhelmed by them. Either way, they lose.

MEN IN MIDLIFE:
LOOKING FOR IDENTITY AND MEANING IN ALL THE WRONG PLACES

When a young man graduates from college he usually jumps into his first job to begin the long arduous climb up the ladder. In many cases he has married, and so in one great juggling act, he is developing his new identity as a young man, forging a new identity (husband), and starting his life's vocation. If children come along he will have an extremely full plate for the next ten to fifteen years. With the bulk of his energy spent trying to keep all of his responsibilities and identities balanced, he has little time to stop, look, listen, and reflect on the quality (or lack of the same) of his life.

For many men it's not until they reach their late thirties or early forties that reality breaks in. Only at this time do many men wake up from what has been a long sleep. They may have already reached many of their goals, or they may realize that they will never reach the goals they had set in their early twenties. In any event, they have started to realize that there is more to life than the treadmill.

Unfortunately, by that time many men are too frightened, too discouraged, or too confused to search for other options. They have already sacrificed their youth, their dreams, the childhoods of their children, their energy, their imagination, and their passion. The satisfaction and pleasure they thought their pursuits would bring have turned out to be like the elusive butterfly.

Though much has been written about the infamous midlife crisis, few have captured better than Dave Barry the absurdities this sense of existential bankruptcy can push people to:

There is virtually no end to the humiliating activities . . . that a man will engage in while in the throes of a mid-life crisis. He will destroy a successful practice as a certified public accountant to pursue a career in Roller Derby. He will start wearing enormous pleated pants and designer fragrances ("Ralph Lauren's Musque de Stud Hombre: For the Man Who Wants A Man Who Smells Vaguely Like A Horse"). He will encase his pale, porky body in tank tops and a "pouch"-style swimsuit the size of a gum wrapper. He will buy a boat shaped like a marital aid. He will abandon his attractive and intelligent wife to live with a 19-year-old aerobics instructor who once spent an entire summer reading a single *Glamour* magazine article entitled "Ten Tips for Terrific Toenails."[7]

Many of you are familiar with the story of middle-aged Mitch as portrayed in the movie *City Slickers*. When we first meet him, he and his two best friends, Phil and Ed, are running down the streets of Pamplona, Spain, being chased by the bulls. Phil and Ed get away, but Mitch isn't quite so lucky. He receives a painful wound that makes it hard for him to sit down for several weeks.

Of course, this isn't the first wild thing these three have done. For several years they have tried to find new, more exotic, and more dangerous ways to both discover and prove their masculinity. On the plane ride home from Spain, Phil shares his idea with the guys for their next adventure. A high-altitude plane jump.

As we get to know Mitch better we find that he's a pretty normal guy. He is married, has two children (a boy and a girl), and has a good job selling air time at a local radio station. By most people's standards he is a successful American male. However, Mitch is depressed and discouraged. He feels helpless and hopeless. He has lost his joy and passion for life.

One day he is asked to go to "Career Day" at his son Danny's school. The dad who precedes him tells exciting stories of his life as a construction worker. The kids are enthralled with his tales of daring, danger, and bravery. Mitch knows that he's up next. He'll have to share the exciting story of his work at a radio station "selling air." When he does get up before the kids here's what he says:

> Value this time in your life, kids, because this is the time in your life when you still have your choices. It goes by so fast.

When you're a teenager, you think you can do anything and you do. Your twenties are a blur.

Thirties you raise your family, you make a little money, and you think to yourself, "What happened to my twenties?"

Forties, you grow a little pot belly, you grow another chin. The music starts to get too loud, one of your old girlfriends from high school becomes a grandmother.

Fifties, you have a minor surgery—you call it a procedure, but it's a surgery.

Sixties, you'll have major surgery, the music is still loud, but it doesn't matter because you can't hear it anyway.

Seventies, you and the wife retire to Fort Lauderdale. You start eating dinner at 2:00 in the afternoon, you have lunch around 10:00, breakfast the night before, spend most of your time wandering around malls looking for the ultimate soft yogurt and muttering, "How come the kids don't call? How come the kids don't call?"

The eighties, you'll have a major stroke, and you end up babbling with some Jamaican nurse who your wife can't stand, but who you call Mama.

Any questions?

Several days later Mitch and his wife, Barbara, are having a discussion. She tells him, "I know you're not happy here. You're not happy at work."

"I just feel lost," Mitch replies.

The family has planned a trip to Florida, but Barbara tells Mitch that she doesn't want him to go to Florida with them. Ed and Phil have invited Mitch to go with them on a cattle drive. "Go away with Ed and Phil," she says. "Go and find your smile."

"What if I can't?" Mitch asks.

After a long pause Barbara responds, "Well, we'll jump off that bridge when we come to it."

There are many men today who have lost their smiles. They have little joy in living. They are not sure where they are and they're even less sure where they are going. There are some good reasons for this crisis. Here are five reasons many men today are at a crossroads.

AN AMBIGUOUS DEFINITION OF MASCULINITY

Do you remember Ted's statement, "I'm not really sure what it means to be a man"? That's a statement that many men today are making. Men in America are faced with conflicting and ambiguous definitions of masculinity. *Ambiguous* means doubtful, uncertain, indistinct, and inexplicable. That's exactly how many men today feel about their identity.

What does it mean to be a man? How do you get there? When do you know that you've arrived? For most of the history of mankind, across centuries and cultures, manhood has been defined by three primary roles: the protector or warrior, the provider or hunter, and the procreator or sire. These were the standards against which men were measured. The success or failure of men was to a great degree dependent upon their ability to protect, provide, and procreate.

Since the Industrial Revolution these three pillars of men's identity have been seriously undermined. For example, with concerns about overpopulation and scientific breakthroughs such as artificial insemination, a man is optional in the little-valued process of procreation.

Furthermore, the increase of women in the work force and the increasing recognition of the competence of women has helped to redefine the man's role as provider. Many men are no longer the sole provider. In fact, in many marriages today the woman makes more than the man does; this can be emotionally catastrophic for the man whose identity rests on earning more than his wife.

A man's role as provider is further undercut by retirement. Economic crises, unemployment, working women, and early retirement have changed his role as the provider.

Yet there remains today a tremendous need for strong and godly men to provide moral and spiritual leadership and nourishment for their wives and children.

THE LACK OF HEALTHY FATHERS AND OTHER MALE ROLE MODELS

One of the most obvious contributors to our crisis in masculinity is the lack of healthy fathers. Many men grew up with dads who were either physically or emotionally unavailable. In many cases they grew up with physically or emotionally absent dads and so had nowhere to learn how to father. This has produced a generation of men without models—men who have little idea of what real masculinity is.

In more than twenty years of counseling I've heard countless men share painful and often heartbreaking stories regarding their relationships, or lack of the same, with their dads. "I never knew my dad." "I could never figure out how to please him, how to gain his approval." "I don't have one memory of my dad hugging me or telling me that he loved me." I've had hundreds of men who have been deeply wounded by emotionally unavailable or physically absent fathers. I've had comparatively few who have suffered from emotionally unavailable or physically absent mothers.

In my counseling practice I have worked with many men, from professional athletes to physicians to ministers, who are very successful in what they do but who, like Ted, are relationally bankrupt. Nowhere is this more evident than in the lack of healthy relationships between most fathers and sons. Everyone has watched professional football and seen the cameras focus on a player who just made a terrific play. The first things he says is, "Hi, Mom!" Do you ever remember hearing a player say, "Hi, Dad"?

Nicholas Davidson says,

Fifteen million American children, one quarter of the population under 18, are growing up today without fathers. This is the greatest social catastrophe facing our country. It is at the root of the epidemics of crime and drugs, it is deeply implicated in the decline in educational attainment, and it is largely responsible for the persistence of widespread poverty despite generous government support for the needy.

Raising a family without a father is not impossible. But it is exceedingly difficult."[8]

Of the 15 million children without fathers, roughly 5.4 million are products of divorce, 3.3 million of marital separation, 4 million of illegitimate birth, with the remainder living with their widowed mothers or neither parent. The absence of fathers is over twice as common as it was a generation ago.[9]

Today many sons have little idea of what their father really does, or if and why it is important. Their father may work an hour from where they live and by the time he returns home at night he is too exhausted for much meaningful parenting. Robert Bly believes that "the love unit most damaged by the Industrial Revolution has been the father-son bond."[10]

In *Iron John*, Robert Bly writes:

As I've participated in men's gatherings since the early 1980's, I've heard one statement over and over from American males, which has been phrased in a hundred different ways: 'There's not enough father.' The sentence implies that father is a substance like salt, which in earlier times was occasionally in short supply, or like the ground water, which in some areas now has completely disappeared.[11]

Bly believes that especially for a boy the results of growing up without a father can be devastating. Even a flawed father can provide masculine images for sons to color in, manly dots to connect. When fatherless boys grow up, he says, they tend to distrust authority and father figures. For their deepest needs, they turn to women. They turn into what Bly calls "soft" or "limp" males who are out of touch with their masculinity and often defer to women in their lives.[12]

In my experience I've seen that one of the best recipes for effective fathering is, like Ward Cleaver in "Leave It to Beaver," to get involved with your kids. It doesn't matter whether you are playing a game of catch, wrestling on the floor, reading a book, or popping into you son's room to see how he's doing. Dads can make a big difference. I've seen that the more time fathers invest in their families, the better off both they and their children will be in later life.

Fathers' family participation also tends to improve their children's lives as young adults. Several studies have suggested that warmth and attention from Dad produce more confident, skillful boys and mature, autonomous girls. Children also are more likely to advance beyond their parents' level of education when their fathers encourage intellectual growth.[13]

Fortunately the current generation of males is beginning to realize the effect this deficit has had on them. An increasing number of dads are enthusiastically hurling themselves into their children's lives. One evidence of this is the number of dads who are intimately acquainted with Big Bird, Bert and Ernie, Oscar the Grouch, and the other lovable characters of "Sesame Street."

Many dads are spending more time reading to their kids. I have fond memories of driving with my good friend Tom Peterson to our psychology internship at the V.A. Hospital in Knoxville, Iowa. We had both spent so much time reading Dr. Suess's *ABC* to our kids that we could both quote it by heart.

LEAVING THE FEMININE TO FIND THE MASCULINE

Another major factor that has brought men to this crossroads involves the important childhood process of developing a separate identity from Mom and Dad and developing one's own identity. This process is more complicated for boys than for girls. As young men we are told we must leave our close ties with our mothers if we are to have any hope of becoming men.

In contrast, girls never have to undo their primary attachment and identification as a woman. They may continue to stay closely attached to their mothers as they form their own unique identities. Boys in our society, in order to develop a male identity, must follow a much more complicated path.

In order to become an individual and reach maturity a boy must, like the girl, separate from his mother. Unlike the girls he must begin to form another sense of gender identity. However, in our culture boys get the message that identification with the feminine is not masculine, so he is pressured to separate not only in his identity but at the deepest levels of relationship. Otherwise he risks being labeled a "Mama's boy." Do you remember how insulting that label would have felt when you were in junior high?

One of the effects of this process is that adult women tend to be more comfortable in relationships and may be frightened by separation. On the other hand, many adult men find their security in independence and are frightened by attachments they don't understand how to handle or they fear may swallow them up and destroy their identity as males. "Since masculinity is defined through separation while femininity is defined through attachment," Carol Gilligan writes, "male gender identity is threatened by intimacy while female gender identity is threatened by separation." This may be one reason most males have problems with relationships and many females tend to have problems with individuation.[14]

THE NEGATIVE EFFECTS OF BOYHOOD SOCIALIZATION

Little boys are different from little girls. And from very early ages they are treated differently. Girls tend to be picked up, held closer and for longer periods of time, allowed to cry, and comforted more than boys. Girls' ability to nurture is itself nurtured and encouraged. When I was in high school the masculinity of any boy who liked to baby-sit was automatically suspect. But girls are encouraged to baby-sit.

When growing up, boys tend to be surrounded by adult women: at home, in the nursery, at school, and at church. They are for the most part nurtured and taught by women. This often leads to them being in a learning environment that, by its very structure, puts them at a disadvantage.

"Today the primary school classroom is a very feminine environment," Aaron Kipnis, a clinical psychologist and specialist on gender issues, explains.

> Neatness, conformity, quietness, politeness, verbal skills, and other historically *feminine* virtues are highly emphasized there. But boys are more active, disorderly, and aggressive, and less verbal, than girls. Consequently boys have greater failure rates and are perceived as having more personality problems in school. Since they're socialized to be more autonomous, they're often less interested in pleasing the teacher than girls are. They're often frustrated by repetitive drills in skills at which they're the weakest. They're labeled as having attention-deficit disorders. But for many reasons it's often harder for boys to sit still in a classroom. They're restless and energetic, not wrong or deviant.[15]

Kipnis says that boys' difficulties in school may indicate how the educational system does not recognize or help the different "styles and modes of learning of boys and girls."

NO CLEAR RITES OF PASSAGE

For thousands of years cultures from around the world have reflected the belief that becoming a real man is not something that just happens. Unlike femininity, which comes naturally through biological maturation, the concept of masculinity has been viewed as something that must be learned, earned, and defended. Anthropologist David Gilmore has researched and summarized a variety of masculinity rituals that are strikingly similar. He has found that

> there is a constantly recurring notion that real manhood is different from simple [physical] maleness, that it is not a natural condition that comes about spontaneously through biological maturation but rather is a precarious or artificial state that boys must win against powerful odds. This recurrent notion that manhood is problematic, a critical threshold that boys must pass through testing, is found at all levels of sociocultural development regardless of what other alternative roles are recognized. It is found among the simplest hunters and fishermen, among peasants and sophisticated urbanized people."[16]

In some cultures certain rituals are demanded of young boys to free them from the feminine. For example to make a Sambian warrior the males begin to spend more time with their sons at four or five years of age. This is the beginning of the process separating the mother and son in order to help him become masculine.

In Sambian culture, as in our own, being a man starts with separation from, and at all costs avoiding, the feminine. The first stage of being a man is demonstrating that you are not a woman. This is definition by negation rather than by affirmation. This is reactive and not proactive.

These rites of passage invariably involve challenges to a boy's physical strength, endurance, and courage. However, with the industrialization and urbanization of our culture, a boy's physical size, strength, and courage have become less a part of our survival needs. The traditional methods for proving masculinity are no longer meaningful or effective for us. Physical strength and bravery are no longer the defining features of men, except perhaps with some adolescent males.

We no longer need to cross wild frontiers, carve homesteads out of the wilderness, plow fields with the muscles of our own bodies. Yes, there are still risky occupations, the majority of which are held by men. Policemen, firemen, test pilots, and soldiers still risk their lives, but these kinds of jobs compose only a small proportion of what men do today.

Today men face different fears: Can I provide for my family? Will I get that promotion? Can I confront my boss? Can I disagree with my wife? Can I take a stand for an unpopular position and face the inevitable rejection and humiliation? These are different kinds of mountains that men have to climb. But they are nonetheless real. They involve a different kind of courage.

Men today face a culture with no rites of passage, no markers, no clearly achievable goals, no guaranteed rewards, no clear standard that they've made it. So we make up our own.

For many the standard is financial success. For some the motto is: If you've got it, flaunt it. A little polo player sewn onto a shirt allows merchants to mark up the selling price 100 percent. It announces to the world that I'm willing to spend two or three times what something is worth because I'm successful, I have the money to spend, and I don't care.

I remember being in Kansas City to speak for a Kansas City Chiefs pregame chapel service. The opposing team was coming into the hotel, and Carrie, my wife, and I noticed one of their star players, an NFL All-Pro, wearing a full-length mink coat.

For some the standard is how busy you are. A man who has arrived is a man who is in demand. He has phones at home, at work, and in his car, and he carries one of the nifty new cellular phones in his pocket.

When he comes to work in the morning, he "complains" about all of the pink phone message slips on his desk. Women know they are important if their man gives them pink roses. Men know they are important if their desk is filled with pink message slips. We have markers of aging such as the first shave, first date, and first car, but our society lacks ceremonial rites. Without clear markers, boys in our culture are required to find the door to manhood on their own.

Men Under Fire

In recent years men have become the targets of all kinds of criticism. We are criticized because we don't listen well, we don't talk enough (especially about our feelings, but, of course, that's because when it comes to feelings we have nothing to talk about), we know how to make love but don't know how to love, we are too easily angered, irresponsible, unfaithful, inconsiderate, untrustworthy, we don't ask for help (until it's too late), we are passive, domineering, don't know how to bond, are selfish, like to play too much, don't know how to parent . . . and the list goes on.

We have been accused of being sexist, but in recent years we have become the butt of feminist humor.

Over the past two years Men's Rights, Inc., has analyzed thousands of print and video ads and compiled annual lists of the best and worst portrayals of men. "What we found was that in almost every instance of a male-female relationship, if one was incompetent it was always the man."

David Rose, president of the National Congress for Men, says the most destructive images involve fathers: "The portrayal of dads being inept affects some important aspects of our lives."

"The women's movement raised consciousness in the ad business as to how women can be depicted," says Fred Danzig, editor of *Advertising Age.* "The thought now is, if we can't have women in these old-fashioned traditional roles, at least we can have men being dummies." Or naked hunks. Or both. Turnabout, say advertising executives, is good business.

A recent article in *Newsweek* entitled "The Ad World's New Bimbos" documents a major shift that has taken place in the advertising world. After decades of selling products by depicting women as anxious half-wits and sultry fantasy objects, advertisers have switched bimbos. Suddenly it is the man's turn to be the bumbling incompetent domestic in need of professional advice or the sex object promoting everything from underwear to Kodak film.

The "male-bashing bonanza" has extended to books, where men are to be controlled, ignored, or endured. For a book on man-and-woman relationships to make the national best-seller list, "women had to look wonderful, as in *Women Who Love Too Much* or *Smart Women: Foolish Choices*; or men had to look like the problem, as in *The Peter Pan Syndrome, The Wendy Dilemma, Smart Women: Foolish Choices*; or at best, peripheral, as in *Men Are Just Desserts*."[17]

Aaron Kipnis has made the clever observation that today we have

> *Smart Women, Foolish Choices* and *Women Who Love Too Much*. There are *Wild Women with Passive Men* and women with *The Cinderella Complex*, who find *No Good Men* while facing the *Don Juan Dilemma* in relationships with men who have *The Peter Pan Complex* or *The Casanova Complex*. They wonder *Should Women Stay with Men Who Stray, Men Who Can't Love*, or *Men Who Cannot Be Faithful*? There are also *Men Who Hate Women and the Women Who Love Them* and *Men Who Hate Women and the Women Who Marry Them*, who have given rise to the *Men Who Hate Themselves and the Women Who Agree with Them*."[18]

Remember some of the "Dumb Blonde" jokes that recently circulated around the country? One day I found in my mailbox at work a list of "Dumb Men" jokes that a woman in one of our women's groups had given to the leader. Here is a sample:

Do you know why all dumb blonde jokes are one liners? So men can understand them.

What is the difference between Government Bonds and Men? Government Bonds mature.

What's the difference between a man and E.T.? E.T. phoned home.

Why is psychoanalysis a lot quicker for men than for women? When it's time to go back to his childhood, he's already there.

How do men define a 50/50 relationship? We cook/they eat; we clean/they dirty; we iron/they wrinkle.

How do men exercise at the beach? By sucking in their stomachs every time they see a bikini.

How are men like noodles? They are always in hot water, they lack taste, and they need dough.

Why is it good that there are female astronauts? When the crew gets lost in space, at least the women will ask for directions.

As I've shared this with groups of men they've laughed, but it's the kind of laugh that includes a bit of pain. Most of these jokes are funny because they contain an element of truth. A truth that has frustrated women for many years. A truth that is another indicator of masculinity at the crossroads.

Many women believe that for years men have had all of the privilege and power, so women don't stand a chance when engaged in conflict with a man. Perhaps in the areas of politics and finances men have had the privilege and power. But when it comes to relationships most men feel vulnerable and one-down. Richard Meth and Robert Pasik write that

> many women feel powerless in conflicts with men, and therefore believe men must feel powerful. However, because men believe they must appear heroic and infallible to women, conflict with a female partner is more likely to leave a man feeling rejected and that he has failed in some way. When men react in anger and with dominating behavior, it is to defend against this threat, rather than from a feeling of power.[19]

It's taken me years to get out of my head and into my heart. I still work at it. Within the past few years I went through an extremely painful experience with someone at work. I discovered that for more than a year someone who I thought was a friend had betrayed my trust. He said one thing to my face and another thing behind my back. Finally God brought things out into the light and his deception and duplicity became public.

Several weeks after this happened one of our senior therapists came into my office and asked, "What are you feeling?"

I responded by saying something like, "I'm feeling pretty good." I went on to talk about my schedule, my writing, and so on.

He listened politely and, after a few minutes came back with, "That's great, but that's not what I asked. What I asked was, 'What are you feeling?'"

I thanked him for caring enough to ask the potentially awkward question, for not letting me stay in my head. I was able to open up and share with him, and we had a good time of prayer together. When he left my office I felt encouraged and refreshed. He had been a friend.

At this point some of you may be saying, "Gary, I know what you're saying is right on. That's what I need to do. But when I experience grief it's too threatening to share it with someone else." That's OK! You are in good company. I've worked with many men who have said exactly the same thing. One of the things they have found helpful is to begin by talking with the Lord, first silently, then out loud in prayer. We all hurt, we all have pain, we've all suffered loss. But where are our choices? What are our options?

Without the passion and intensity our emotions were designed to give us, many men become paralyzed by the very emotions they ignore and deny. They exchange their backbone for a wishbone. Rather than attending "wildman" gatherings, they look for "mildman" gatherings.

His nickname is "Stormin' Norman," but General Schwarzkopf prefers his other nickname: "The Bear." If you had a chance to see Barbara Walter's wonderful interview with him on March 15, 1991, you saw a man who was a competent, effective, strong, "typically male" kind of guy. You also saw a man who wept with great dignity and grace when asked about having to leave his family behind to go off to the Persian Gulf War and wept again when asked about the families of his troops. He is a man who likes the opera and had pictures of family members all over his humble quarters in Saudi Arabia. He shared that he has been scared in every war he's been in. And this tough, perhaps crusty, four-star general said right on national television that *a man who can't cry scares him.* By all accounts, Schwarzkopf embodies a man who has both fierceness and tenderness.

If we are becoming "godly men," we will be "man" enough to

- take an honest look at ourselves from God's perspective (mind, will, and emotions).
- have our lives characterized by the fruit of the Spirit.
- say, "I was wrong, I'm sorry, will you forgive me?"
- face and deal with our own issues and allow God to heal our wounds.
- become accountable to some other men.
- love and accept those who are different from us. We can disagree with what people do and still see them as having infinite worth and value.
- risk becoming passionate men who aren't afraid to love.
- risk being tender as well as tough, to acknowledge that there is nothing as strong as gentleness and nothing as gentle as real strength.
- model the fact that sometimes we stand tallest when we are on our knees.
- have the courage to care, commit, make a promise . . . and keep it!

NOTES

1. Ronald F. Levant, "Toward the Reconstruction of Masculinity," *Journal of Family Psychology* 5, no. 3–4 (March/June 1992): 379–402.
2. Herbert Goldberg, *The New Male: From Self-Destruction to Self-Care* (New York: William Morrow, 1979), 13.
3. Ibid., 20–21, 44, 218; Aaron Kipnis, *Knights Without Armor* (Los Angeles: Tarcher, 1991), 11–34, 47, 57, 159; Daniel Evan Weiss, *The Great Divide: How Females and Males Really Differ* (New York: Poseidon, 1991).
4. Search Institute: *Source* 4, no. 4 (December 1988): 66, 83–88, 126–28, 135–40, 147–51; P. Benson, D. Williams, and A. Johnson, *The Quicksilver Years: The Hopes and Fears of Early Adolescence* (San Francisco: Harper & Row, 1987).
5. P. Benson, P. Wood, A. Johnson, C. Eklin, J. Mills, *Minnesota Survey on Drug Use and Drug-Related Attitudes* (Minneapolis: Search Institute, 1983).
6. Frank Pittman, "The Masculine Mystique," *Networker* (May/June 1990): 50–51.
7. Dave Barry, *Dave Barry Turns 40* (New York: Crown, 1990), 75–76.
8. Nicholas Davidson, "Life Without Father: America's Greatest Social Catastrophe," in *Policy Review* 51, The Heritage Foundation (Winter 1990): 40.
9. Ibid.
10. Robert Bly, *Iron John: A Book About Men* (New York: Vintage, 1990), 19.
11. Ibid.
12. Ibid., 1–4.
13. "The Benefits of Fatherhood," *Psychology Today* (March 1989), 76.
14. Carol Gilligan, *In a Different Voice: Psychological Theory and Women's Development* (Cambridge, Mass.: Harvard Univ., 1982), 8.
15. Kipnis, *Knights Without Armor*, 257.
16. David Gilmore, *Mankind in the Making: Cultural Concepts of Masculinity* (New Haven, Conn.: Yale Univ., 1990), 11.
17. Warren Farrell, *Why Men Are the Way They Are* (New York: McGraw-Hill, 1986), 203.
18. Kipnis, *Knights Without Armor*, 65–66.
19. Richard L. Meth and Robert S. Pasick, *Men in Therapy: The Challenge of Change* (New York: Guilford, 1990), 198.

If you would like more tools in facing the crisis of masculinity, pick up the Moody book *Real Men Have Feelings Too*.

Moody Press, a ministry of the Moody Bible Institute, is designed for education, evangelization, and edification. If we may assist you in knowing more about Christ and the Christian life, please write us without obligation: Moody Press, c/o MLM, Chicago, Illinois 60610.